MY COMMUNITY

A TRIP TO THE BALL GAME

Kirsten Lake

PowerKiDS press.

New York

Published in 2017 by The Rosen Publishing Group, Inc.
29 East 21st Street, New York, NY 10010

First Edition

Editor: Melissa Raé Shofner
Book Design: Mickey Harmon

Photo Credits: Cover, pp. 5, 15, 22 Blend Images - Kevin Dodge/Getty Images; p. 7 Sean Pavone/Shutterstock.com; p. 9 Hans Neleman/Getty Images; p. 11 Chuck Meyers/Shutterstock.com; pp. 13, 17 Suzanne Tucker/Shutterstock.com; p. 19 tammykayphoto/Shutterstock.com; p. 21 Monkey Business Images/Shutterstock.com.

Cataloging-in-Publication Data

Names: Lake, Kirsten.
Title: A Trip to the ball game / Kirsten Lake.
Description: New York : PowerKids Press, 2017. | Series: My community | Includes index.
Identifiers: ISBN 9781499427820 (pbk.) | ISBN 9781499430004 (library bound) | ISBN 9781508152910 (6 pack)
Subjects: LCSH: Baseball--Juvenile literature.
Classification: LCC GV867.5 L35 2017 | DDC 796.357--d23

Manufactured in the United States of America

CPSIA Compliance Information: Batch #BW17PK: For Further Information contact Rosen Publishing, New York, New York at 1-800-237-9932

CONTENTS

We play baseball at the ballpark.

A ballpark has four **bases**.

Our team has nine players.

The **baseball** is white.

Players throw the ball.
Players catch the ball.

The batter wears a **helmet**.

I hit the ball with a bat.

I run around the bases.
Homerun!

Our families cheer!

Baseball is fun!

WORDS TO KNOW

baseball

bases

helmet

INDEX

WEBSITES

Due to the changing nature of Internet links, PowerKids Press has developed an online list of websites related to the subject of this book. This site is updated regularly. Please use this link to access the list: www.powerkidslinks.com/mycom/ball